The Miracle
of Bolckow

David Page

For more information, please contact:

Open Door Christian Center
400 Seventh Street
Bolckow, MO 64427
www.OpenDoorCC.org

ISBN-10:1720865183
ISBN-13:978-1720865186

DEDICATION

We give thanks and praise to God our Father, the
Lord Jesus Christ, and the Holy Spirit,
without Whom none of this would be possible.

We give all of the glory to You!

CONTENTS

WHY YOU SHOULD READ THIS BOOK

The world needs God today.

People have questions about God. Is He real? Does He answer prayers? Are miracles for today?

Even in the church today, there is much confusion about God. This book cannot answer all of these questions, but if you are searching, this book provides you with true stories from real people who share how God changed their life in a most unlikely place in northwest Missouri.

This is the story of a church in a place called Bolckow, a town with a current population of 187. Open Door Christian Center is an interdenominational church and has consistently grown over the last ten years.

It is the story of a minister whom God sent to a church in 2007, to pastor sixteen people. This book records some of the miraculous events in the life of this church and its members and visitors.

If you are a person searching for God or a Christian wanting more of God, this book is for you!

The testimony of this church and its people will inspire you and give you the confidence that God is still moving supernaturally today.

Preface

It is a great privilege for me to be sharing with you the stories of how God has come to a small town in rural America and revealed His presence.

The Lord had been dealing with me for several years to write this book. It is the story of a church that was born in 1993, that grew for a time and then began to decline.

A revival is needed when something is dying or has died. In 2007, God began reviving the church and today it is a vibrant community of believers in Jesus Christ.

The book is also a helpful reminder for those who have experienced the supernatural workings of God and to encourage those that may not have. God is faithful and He has not changed. He is still doing the same works that He was doing 2,000 years ago in the Book of Acts.

Jesus Christ is the same yesterday, and today, and forever.

(Hebrews 13:8)

For the title of this book we are defining a "miracle" as a supernatural work of God. This word may be used to describe a healing, a baptism in the Holy Spirit, or a supernatural encounter that reveals the God of the Bible.

The stories that are included are those that were provided to us from real people with real stories. Their testimonies were either shared publicly at an Open Door event or written by the individual and given to us to share. Regretfully, there are many stories and events that have occurred at the church that were not able to be included in this book. There are so many testimonies!

The reasons for sharing them are threefold:

1. To give glory to God.
2. To show thankfulness for what the Lord did for them.
3. To encourage those reading them to grow in their faith, that God is still loving and healing people today.

There has been some minor editing to bring clarity and some of the names have been changed, altered or removed for privacy and safety. Nothing has been added to embellish their stories or to exaggerate any of their claims.

It is the author's desire that this book represents what God has been doing in Bolckow and that our Lord Jesus Christ gets *all* the glory for what *He has done!*

As this book goes to print, the church will be celebrating its 25th Anniversary. Many lives have been touched, healed and blessed by the Word of God and the move of the Holy Spirit in this small town.

To all those who consider Open Door to be their church home, there is no greater privilege for me as a minister of the Gospel to say, it is an honor to serve the Lord with you in Bolckow, Missouri. Thank you to all of you who courageously shared what God has done and is continuing to do in your lives.

For those of you that are about to read this book, we pray that it will encourage you and strengthen your faith that God is still in the "miracle" business.

David Page

PART ONE:
In the Beginning, God...

Chapter 1

"It's Time for You to Leave"

I heard a still, small voice say, "It's time for you to leave" as I entered the ramp for US Hwy 169 in Owasso. My response was simple... "Get thee behind me, Satan!"

It was March of 2007 as I was driving to my place of employment in Collinsville, Oklahoma. I was privileged to be on the staff at "A Glorious Church Fellowship", under the leadership and guidance of Pastor Lee Morgans and his wife Jan.

Everything was going well. My wife, Pamela, was also working in Collinsville and we had purchased our first home together in another town nearby.

Life was good! Everything was going well ... surely God would not wish me to leave this wonderful church family and ministry.

Through my previous experiences with God, deep down I

knew that what I had heard was the leading of the Holy Spirit... I just didn't want to hear it or accept it!

Many people have difficulty with the idea that God speaks to us and guides us. However, Scripture clearly reveals God's guidance to those that know Him. It was Jesus who said, *"My sheep listen to my voice; I know them, and they follow me"* (John 10:27).

As time passed, I would continue to pray for the Lord's will for my life. Again and again I heard that still, small voice saying, "It's time for you to leave". After the third time, I asked for guidance as to what I should do.

At this moment in time, Pamela and I had no savings and we had no other financial support system, other than working with our hands and trusting God to bless our work. In other words no work... no money... no food!

We also know that God is our Source and that God's provision follows His vision. So I started praying about the next step. It was during this time that I received no direction except an occasional, "It's time for you to leave".

I was stuck! At this point I had not discussed anything about this with Pamela. I had no answers and I did not wish to worry my wife.

It was now April of 2007. I had now realized that the Lord was waiting for me to resign from my current position and to trust Him for the next step!

I needed to talk to Pamela! I wasn't sure how she would react? I shared with her what I felt the Lord was guiding me to do. Pam just looked at me and said, "If you feel like the Lord wants you to resign, then go ahead. We'll be fine."

I reminded her that if we get this wrong we could lose the house in three months. Pam's response was, "That's okay, it will be fine!"

I called my family in England and spoke with my Mum. I told her the same as what I had shared with Pamela. To my surprise her response was, "It's okay, God has a plan," and she was excited!

This was crazy or God!

As many of you may know, one of the important needs of most wives is financial security. And the two most influential women in my life were just agreeing with each other... "Go ahead, quit your job!"

On Sunday, April 15, 2007, I visited with my pastor and handed in my resignation.

Now we were praying!

Not just praying, but really praying... "Lord, show us the next step."

It was one week later; on Friday, April 20th while sleeping, I had a dream. In this dream I saw the words "Open Door Ministries." I wrote this down on a notepad. As I switched the lamp off I noticed that the time was 2:30 am and went back to sleep.

In the morning, I searched the internet and newspapers for anything that resembled Open Door Ministries and a job, but to no avail. I continued to pray.

Another week was passing and after prayer on the following Thursday evening (April 26th), I felt an urge to check the Rhema Bible Training Center's website for job opportunities.

Wow, there it was!

"Open Door Ministries" and the job description was me! The only question left was...

"Where's Bol-cow?"

Chapter 2

"Where's Bol-cow?"

If you have seen the children's books "Where's Waldo?", you will understand the humor of this expression.

In the children's books, Waldo is a character hidden among hundreds of other people and you have to find him. This is similar to Bolckow as a place in the thousands of towns and cities in the United States. No one has heard of it!

Bolckow is actually pronounced "Bol-coe'" and is a small town in rural America. It currently has a population of 187 and is located between St. Joseph and Maryville in Missouri off of Highway 71.

Bolckow was established in 1868 and became a thriving community due to the expansion of the railroad. However, in 1967 after heavy rains, a railway bridge was washed out and that ended the freight service through Bolckow. This affected the prosperity of this once thriving town. People began leaving and the population began to decline.

Even today, the main road into the town from the highway can be flooded if there are heavy rains.

When we arrived in 2007, there was just a post office and two churches with small congregations in the town. Access to the internet was available by using the "dial-up" internet service offered by the local telephone company.

Our First Visit

We decide to visit Bolckow on the weekend of Saturday, May 5, 2007 and to stay for the Sunday morning service.

It was a hot, sunny day and the journey took about five hours from our home. We were staying in a hotel in Maryville overnight, so we stopped into Bolckow on the way to have a quick peek at the church.

The church was meeting in an old elementary school. The property had an old three-story building and a single-story gymnasium. The property looked like it needed some serious repairs.

As I continued to look around the grounds I could see an old car upside down on the front lawn of a neighbor's house!

It was then that I had noticed that Pamela was already back in the car.

Meanwhile on the parking lot, the Lord was speaking to me...

"Will you come to Bolckow?", He spoke to my heart.

"No!" was my immediate reaction.

This was the first time in my Christian life that my response to God was "No!"

The next few moments were priceless as the Lord revealed His heart and my heart. Once I could see His heart for Bolckow, I repented and changed my answer to "Yes".

We continued on our journey to Maryville. We had done some research on homes in the area and we had decided to look at some rental properties.

As we were looking at one of the properties, we were greeted by a bold, smiling lady who we learned was named Kathy. She started asking us many questions and all of a sudden she asked me, "Are you a pastor?"

I hesitated, because I was sweaty, unshaven and dressed in a t-shirt, shorts and a ball cap. We had just driven five hours from Oklahoma!

I confirmed that I was... and then she said, "I thought so! We as believers should know when we are in the presence of our pastors."

I thought to myself, *Wow! What faith!*

We left after being introduced to her husband Jim, and drove away wondering what the rest of this weekend would be like. (Years later, Kathy and Jim visited Open Door and became members.)

We stayed in Maryville overnight. That night, there was a serious storm and torrential rain. By the morning, the main road to Bolckow was flooded. We had to find the way to Bolckow using the backroads... not a great start! Ironically, every song we sang in worship that morning had to do with rain!

Cecil, one of the elders, shared the message that morning, with about eleven people in attendance including children. Afterwards, we met everyone and had a brief tour of the facilities.

The discussion with Pamela on our way home to Oklahoma was interesting. Everything in the natural, the facilities, the geographical position of the church, the lack of finances was shouting, "Don't go to Bolckow!"

However, we had an unusual peace about the situation. We had to continue to test the leading of the Lord more.

We traveled back and forth to Bolckow a few more times. The church prayed and offered me the position of pastor. The salary was $100 per week.

We accepted. For six months, we traveled every two weeks to the church to preach and teach the Word of God.

We would travel up on Saturday morning and arrive about 3 pm. Virgil and Carol Stanton set up their RV camper for us in Bolckow, where we could rest and stay overnight and then minister on Sunday morning.

Following lunch with the church, we would travel back to our home in Oklahoma.

Our House Sold in Five Days!

During this time of traveling, a local Christian woman named Shirley, heard the news that the new pastor in Bolckow was looking for a home. She contacted the church to see if the new pastor would like to rent hers. She owned a house in Savannah which is a town about fifteen minutes south of Bolckow.

We walked around the home after church one Sunday and it seemed like the Lord's hand was at work. We agreed to rent the home.

Upon returning to Oklahoma, we placed our house on the market and it was sold for the full asking price in five days.

Within a month we were moving to northwest Missouri!

We arrived in Savannah, Missouri on Saturday, September 22, 2007.

Chapter 3

The History of Open Door

Every church has a story. The universal or worldwide Church is a group of people who have become part of the family of God through faith in Jesus Christ. A local church is the family of God coming together to worship in a local setting.

Just as families have stories, so do churches.

In life, natural families have good and bad times. This is the same for churches as they are made up of natural families coming together to worship God and to learn about being part of God's family.

In both families, there are good times and not-so-good times. Good decisions are made and some mistakes are made.

If we are honest with ourselves, when you put any two people together, it is rare to find 100% agreement, 100% of the time.

Have you ever met a perfect husband or wife? What about a perfect mom or dad?

No, as humans, we recognize the weaknesses of humanity.

We experience these weaknesses when we reflect on the ups and downs of marriage, of parenting and in families.

Some of these people are also in God's family, and therefore go to church.

Today, we can see dysfunction in every area of human life. As a minister and a leader in the church, I understand that the birth of a church is similar to that of the birth of a child in a family.

Both the parents and the children have to learn to grow in their roles and walk in love and understanding. The same is true of a church. Both leaders and members of the congregation have to learn to grow and walk in love and understanding.

Unfortunately, for some people, both Christians and non-Christians are less forgiving to people in the church than they are of their own family members. They can leave churches upset at the leadership and sometimes also at God, but they forget that the church is simply made up of regular families in a local area who desire to know God. Some of these people may be parents. I am sure they are glad that their spouses or children didn't leave the family because of their inexperience in leading the members of their family!

Why do I share this?

When a family decides to have children, it is fun to take part in creating the children, but not so much fun in bringing forth the child at delivery. (Ask any mother!)

As soon as the child is born, life gets messy. The changing of the diapers, the sleepless nights, etc. And this is the first few weeks!

In front of the parents are at least eighteen years of training and financing the child, preparing them to leave home. Many mistakes are made by the parents and the children. What is important is that everyone learns from their mistakes.

The same is true in the family of God, the local church. Everyone must learn from their mistakes, to become better Christians and better church leaders.

Yes, the road can be bumpy... but it's worth it!

As you read the history of Open Door, it is like looking at a new family, with new parents learning as they go.

Join with me as we journey back in time, twenty-five years ago to 1993, when the church began because a group of Christians wanted more of God, more of the Holy Spirit and more of the Word of God.

The Early Years (1993 – 2007)

A small group of believers began meeting on Sundays at the Virgil Stanton home for Bible study led by Brad McIntyre. The group was comprised mainly of members of the Stanton family, their spouses and children. Soon, other family members joined, followed by friends and neighbors.

During these meetings, a discussion was made to start a church that was willing to allow the Holy Spirit to move and reign. Calvin West, an Assembly of God minister, was voted in as the pastor in July of 1993. During this time the church was meeting in Virgil and Carol Stanton's garage.

The Name "Open Door"

After a time of prayer and fasting, the group came together to decide on a name for the church. Four names had been chosen.

As those present tried to decide on one, the large garage door opened on its own. Someone got up and closed it and the discussion continued. Again, the garage door opened and again it was closed.

The discussion continued again and a third time the door opens. Two of the people present spoke in unison, "I believe we just got our name." All the other names were thrown out and everyone agreed it was to be Open Door.

The Church begins to Grow

In 1996, the church was legally incorporated.

After approximately seven months, Pastor West left the church and Brad McIntyre was voted in to become the next pastor.

The mission of the church began to evolve. The members began serving the community around them.

One of the ministries in operation was a "clothes closet". A couple in the church offered their house to be used for this purpose. Many winter coats, shoes and other articles of clothing were given out to help people who were in need.

Some of the church members also helped with the local Christian television station Trinity Broadcasting Network, now more widely known as TBN. They volunteered to answer phones, operate TV cameras and be part of TBN's prayer line.

A few events held at the church were Pioneer Days which was held in the fall of 1996 and Frontier Days in the fall of 1999. Some of the members dressed as American patriarchs such as Abraham Lincoln and Betsy Ross. Church services were also held outside, just as it was in those days.

Looking for a Church Home

By 1999, the members of Open Door were looking to "stretch the tent". They began to pray and search for land or a building for the church to meet in.

In 1993, the North Andrew school district had moved into a new school. The old school building in Bolckow became available for purchase in 1994. The church had put a bid in for the property, but at that time the bid was unsuccessful.

Open Door still needed a building and a fund was started in order to finance the purchase of a building or land to build on. The leadership still believed that God wanted them to have the old school. The church continued to pray about a building or land.

In 1999, by word-of-mouth, the church learned that the current owner of the old high school wanted to sell.

One Sunday evening at a service, the people of Open Door prayed that God would provide the school for His work.

In a very short time, the owner of the school contacted the church and wanted to know if the church would like to buy the building.

In March of 1999, the church was in agreement to buy the old high school. With $4,000 already in the building fund another $10,000 was donated. Two years later, the adjoining ball field was also acquired.

The old high school became the new home for Open Door!

The buildings needed to be upgraded. The work needed on the building was immense, including the need for a new roof on the gymnasium. With all of the ministries, Bible studies and regular services and the work on the property, church life became very busy.

On January 6, 2002, Pastor Brad resigned from the church.

The Search for a New Pastor

The church began to pray and search for a pastor. Advertisements were placed in the newspaper and candidates were interviewed.

The church elders took turns giving the message on Sunday morning, with other ministers coming in to preach about once a month.

The next five years were tough on the leadership of the church as the membership continued to dwindle. But they kept searching for a pastor.

During a neighbor's home Bible study, a suggestion was

made to advertise on the website at Rhema Bible Training Center in Broken Arrow, Oklahoma. Gina, who was an elder's wife, placed an announcement on their website for a pastor.

A number of pastors responded and were interviewed. David Page, who was an Englishman as well as an assistant pastor in Oklahoma, responded by email and visited two or three times on the phone.

After more fasting and praying on both sides, there was a unanimous vote by the people and David became our pastor in June of 2007.

At that time, the official membership consisted of twelve adults and four children.

Chapter 4

A New Beginning

*"Unless the Lord builds the house,
they labor in vain who build it"
Psalms 127:1*

In October 2007, things began to change! Pam and I had moved to Missouri and were beginning to settle in. We had weekly services and board meetings. This gave me much time to study, pray and prepare and seek the Lord about His church.

Financially, the church was in debt due to a new roof that was put on the gymnasium. In 2007, every room in the building needed some kind of upgrade, including the bathrooms. Heating and air-conditioning was also needed.

The gymnasium was heated by gas infrared heaters, which were not very effective. Those heaters were only designed to heat objects and not air. In those early years during the winter, people would use blankets to keep warm!

In the summer, with no air conditioning, it was like a sauna. We would just sweat and watch the humidity drip down the concrete walls!

We had begun holding Sunday morning services in the old gymnasium of the school. We had some old pews and plastic picnic chairs for seating, enough for approximately thirty to forty people.

As we entered 2008, we had some good news. A couple in the church wanted to get married. The bad news was that they would need seating for around 150 people! I began to pray...

God Provides!

One Thursday morning, I was walking through the house and I heard the Lord say "Call Pastor Lee." I knew instantly that it was about the chairs.

I called the church office immediately and to my surprise, Pastor Lee answered the phone. The conversation went something like this...

Pastor David: "Hi Pastor Lee, what are you doing answering the phone?"

Pastor Lee: "Linda [the church secretary] is at the dentist, I said I would cover her this morning."

Pastor David: "Well great, anyways I was calling to speak to you. I know you were looking to have new chairs in the sanctuary... Is there any chance you might consider selling the old ones to us?"

Pastor Lee: "I'm sorry David, but last night I gave

them away".

My heart dropped and I thought... I don't hear God anymore!!

Pastor Lee continued. He said "Yes, last night I told the church that we were sending all our old chairs to Pastor David in Bolckow!"

Wow. You can imagine the rest of the conversation and how thankful I am for a pastor that also hears the voice of the Lord!

While we were planning for the wedding, I was also still seeking the Lord about what He wanted to do with Open Door.

The first big instruction I received by the leading of the Holy Spirit, was to hold a tent meeting on the ball field at the church.

During my prayer times, I had also seen in a vision of the placement of the tent which had a blue and white striped top. The date for the event was to be the 23rd of April (2008).

With much excitement, I shared the vision at the next board meeting. I always remember someone saying... "But Pastor, the weather can be cold around here at that time of the year. Can we change the date?"

As an Englishman in northwest Missouri, I had no idea of the extremes of weather in the area. As we left the meeting, we agreed to pray over changing the date.

A week later, we met together and I confirmed that this was to be the date. If this date was not okay, then I felt we should not proceed further at this time. The board unanimously voted to go forward with the tent meeting.

On Saturday, April 12, 2008 we facilitated our first wedding with the new chairs given to us by Pastor Lee and A Glorious Church Fellowship. This was eight days before the tent meeting. As the ceremony began, one of the ushers came up to me to let me know it was snowing outside!

I smiled and thought, *Do we need to order heaters for the tent meeting?!*

The tent went up the following week on Friday… it was wet and cold and this did not look good.

However, the tent company did put the tent up in the exact spot I saw in the vision.

Hmm… I wonder….

The First Tent Meeting

The outside tent revival services were to begin on the evening of Sunday, April 20th and would continue through Wednesday, April 23rd. The weather, the week before, was looking like it would be wet and cold. By Saturday, April 19th at midday, the temperature had reached just over 50 degrees Fahrenheit.

Our first miracle occurred on Sunday, April 20th. The weather had completely changed. By 6 pm, the temperature had reached 75 degrees! This good weather and temperatures carried us through the tent revival services, which had approximately fifty people in attendance during the evening meetings.

When I look back to this tent meeting, I can say it was a

turning point for Open Door. Those that attended experienced a move of the Holy Spirit that you cannot duplicate!

We saw people receive the baptism in the Holy Spirit, and saw many get healed. We also saw people receive and operate in the gifts of the Spirit.

One evening, the Holy Spirit moved upon our children first. I still remember it like it was yesterday.

As I was preaching, a ten-year-old sitting on the front row began giggling! It wasn't long before joy and laughter filled the tent! This wasn't just laughter or happiness, it was deeper. It was coming from the innermost parts of the belly, like rivers of living water. "HA, HA, HA!" was the phrase that stirred the congregation.

Apparently, the young girl was so full of joy; she kept her sisters up until 3 am.

During these services, God was doing something in the people that attended, but He was also doing something over the Bolckow area.

Yes, there were some spectacular God-moments.

Here are some of the testimonies that we received from these meetings:

I would just like to say that it broke my heart to see my daughter leave the park and come to the Monday night service on her own will. She was also intrigued and asked if we could come back the rest of the week. I just want to thank the Lord for making her hungry for the things of God!

- Josh S., St Joseph, Missouri

Sunday, April 20th, I went forward to receive healing for a cold, and I received much more. Yes, I received a healing but I also received the healing gift in my hands, also boldness and much joy.

Tuesday evening, I heard 3 different times the jingle of a bell (in the tent) like that, that sheep wear around their necks.

My sheep listen to my voice; I know them, and they follow me. - John 10:27

All week watching the church receive the gift of tongues, gift of healing in their hands, healing on their body, baptized in the Holy Ghost, the church pressing through the demonic and joy, joy, joy.

On Thursday, Friday and Saturday I realized I had a new love for the Word. It's now alive and understandable to me like never before.

- Carol S., Bolckow, Missouri

Pain in my left side was healed.

- Robert W., Bolckow, Missouri

On the 22nd of April, 2008 in the Tuesday morning service I had an utterance [in an unlearned language/tongues] from the Holy Ghost and then was able to interpret it:

"There is freedom in Jesus . . . you will find unimaginable freedom in the Lord. The Lord will save, the Lord will set you free."

(Galatians 5:1 Stand fast therefore in the liberty by which Christ has made us free, and do not be entangled again with a yoke of bondage.)

- Keith T, Bolckow, Missouri

On Wednesday morning, my daughter Liberty was sick so I came by myself. Pastor David said he and Pamela would come over [to our house] to lay hands on her. By the end of the meeting, I had burning in my right hand and Pastor David said he wouldn't need to come over, that Liberty would be healed.

I was given the gift of healing that day. When I got home and prayed with Liberty she seemed better, but we went ahead and took her to the doctor.

The doctor said there was nothing to be concerned about. Everything would be fine.

- Sommer T, Bolckow, Missouri

There was much intercessory prayer for this event. We also received this testimony from England...

You might be interested in the picture God gave me before the tent meetings began.

There were two flags lying at half-mast over a marquee. One was black and the other brightly colored, the black one went up its pole and waved above the tent but was hauled down and the colored one flew in its place.

They were level at one point but eventually the colored one flew in glorious victorious splendor - Jesus is Lord!!

- Jean K., England, United Kingdom

When I reflect back over the last ten years, we may never know how important this event was. It was a new beginning for a small group of believers.

What would be next?

Chapter 5

Where the Spirit of the Lord is, There is Freedom

Following the first tent meeting, the Holy Spirit began to draw people to Open Door for both spiritual restoration and emotional and physical healing.

It took me around six months to recognize what the Holy Spirit was leading me to do. I had discovered that many people, including Christians, had a distorted view of God and His character.

There is a belief based on church tradition that can be passed down through denominational churches, that Christianity is a good way of life or a good philosophy to live by.

However, true Christianity is much more than this!

It is a way of life that brings people in touch with their Creator, our Father in Heaven. Being a Christian is about having a living relationship with God.

I always remember an important moment for me with one of our older members who has since passed into Heaven. Her name was Beverly. She said:

"I have been taught for fifty years that God will punish me, and now you're trying to tell me that He loves me?!"

Beverly's question helped me to see some of the misunderstood foundations of the faith preached in this area. The Lord began giving me sermons to reveal the true God of the Bible that says that yes, "He is just" but also affirms that "He is love".

The good news is that God is not looking to punish us... He's looking to bless us!

> **For God so loved the world that He gave His only begotten Son,** that **whoever believes in Him should not perish** but have everlasting life.
> - John 3:16

God is a good, good Father! God is more like a loving Father who loves His child.

The Father loves the child, but if the child does something wrong, the Father does not stop loving him or her. He loves the child, but hates the disobedience!

This foundation was important for our church *(and is important for the Body of Christ as a whole).*

Christianity is not a religion with a list of "do's" and "don'ts". True Christianity is about having a good relationship with God that was made possible because of what Jesus did at the cross!

Christianity is not about mankind trying to "work at being good" to obtain God's favor. Instead, the true Gospel is that God has provided the way to a relationship with Him, by grace, when we place our faith in His Son, Jesus Christ.

<u>For it is by grace you have been saved</u>, through faith — and this not from yourselves, it is the gift of God— not by works, so that no one can boast.
                                        - Ephesians 2:8-9 NIV

Below is a wonderful, true story of how God changed a young lady's life, when she understood the true Gospel of Jesus Christ.

I met my husband about 12 years ago and at that time I knew there was a God, but I definitely was not living right!

As a child, I was forced to go to a Catholic church but was able to make my mind up not to continue to go at age twelve. My dad claims to be Methodist but has never been to church. My husband was younger than me and his parents were adamant about going to church, and the only way I could see him was to go to church with him, so I did. It was very strange for me because I only knew the Catholic ways. We ended up getting married and I got pregnant.

My life began to change a lot. His aunt would talk to me a lot about living right and the Bible. I started feeling the need to go back to the church and find out more about my husband's beliefs and those of his family.

There was no pastor at that time and my husband's dad and grandfather led the services that were more like Bible studies. I was learning, so I kept going. My favorite part of the service was the praise and worship. It made me feel something that I never felt before.

After I had my oldest daughter I decided that I wanted to let Jesus into my heart. I called my mother-in-law and

31

told her I loved Jesus and I wanted to be baptized. We began crying together on the phone and the next Sunday I was baptized. This was also the first time my father-in-law told me he loved me! I continued to go to church every Sunday even though there was not a pastor because I just felt right and at home. They taught me the importance of having faith and that God would take care of us.

A few years had passed and I was divorced. I stopped going to church due to being pregnant and having a toddler with no job or money living in St. Joe. I fell away from God because I felt angry, unloved and abandoned. I didn't go back to church for several years.

In the summer of 2008 I believe it was, I met Pastor David and Pam. My sister was having trouble and I contacted my ex-mother-in-law for prayer. She informed me that the church had a pastor and I need to contact him. I was hesitant at first, but I did call.

He and his wife wanted to meet with my sister and I. We set up a time and met them at their house.

They prayed with my sister, while I sat in the background. I sat quietly, guarded for fear of being hurt or rejected and I didn't want to open up to anyone or anything.

As they prayed for my sister, I began to cry, because that was the first time I felt like I heard God tell me He loved me, but I was still very guarded and didn't want to be prayed for.

As we, my sister and I, left the house, I can remember looking back out of my rearview mirror and seeing them standing in the doorway to the house watching us pull *away. I remember thinking that maybe they were ok and really do care.*

I kept in touch with Pastor David and Pam after that and started coming back to the church. I have been back to Open Door ever since and became free in Jesus Christ. I have learned my value to Him and that He really does love me. Today I'm still a single mom working as an LPN. Times do get rough but I know now that God will never leave me and I can do all things through Him which gives me strength!

Tasha M.
St. Joseph, Missouri

Everything we do at Open Door, from church services, kids programs and community events, we do to help people connect with God that they may know Him.

We have held movie nights, community events, kid's evangelistic crusades, revival services and conferences. From all of these events, there are hundreds of people who have been to Open Door and have given their life to Jesus or have rededicated their life to Him.

Here is another person's story, as they shared their story on a Sunday morning in front of the congregation:

I'm a little nervous, so, I don't speak in front of people very often . . . , but last week, I said . . . the salvation prayer and I accepted Jesus Christ into my heart . . .

So, I guess I can kind of tell you how I got up here, and . . . it was actually my mom and I had a conversation, I think it was about a couple years ago, and it just kind of hit us at once that we were kind of missing something . . . you know,

33

there was an emptiness that we both had felt and . . . this was, this is probably my fifth church that I've attended in the last year so and . . .

I really like all the people here and as soon as I, as soon as I walked in, I didn't feel like people were judging me, you know, I was accepted and so that made it a lot easier for me to accept Jesus Christ into my heart.

As you read these stories, you may be thinking "I want that" or "I want to know God like that." The good news is that you can. If God will touch one person, it reveals His will to touch others. God *really* wants a close relationship with you!

This is why God sent Jesus, to open the door for mankind to have a relationship with Him, to open the door to Heaven for us. Before Jesus came, the door was not open. But after Jesus came and paid the penalty for our sins, the door was opened. Jesus shared these insights with His disciples. We are able to read about them in the Gospel of John:

> *(Jesus speaking)* **I am the door. If anyone enters by Me, he will be saved,** and will go in and out and find pasture.
>
> - John 10:9

> Jesus said to him, "I am the way, the truth, and the life. **No one comes to the Father except through Me.**"
>
> - John 14:6

The only way to God is through Jesus. This is why we need Jesus. Your faith in Jesus and what He has done for you opens the door to Heaven!

The people in the Bible (Acts 2:37-39) asked the question: "What shall we do?"

Peter replied, "Repent and be baptized, every one of you, in the name of Jesus Christ for the forgiveness of your sins. And you will receive the gift of the Holy Spirit.

> As the Scripture says, **"Anyone who trusts in him will never be put to shame."** For there is no difference between Jew and Gentile — **the same Lord is Lord of all and richly blesses all who call on him,** for, **"Everyone who calls on the name of the Lord will be saved."**
> - Romans 10:11-13 NIV

Are you ready to call on Him?

To call on God, is like making a call on a cell phone. It is talking to someone. When we talk to God, we call that prayer.

A simple, personal prayer from you to God is all that is needed, like the one below:

Dear Heavenly Father,
I am sorry for the things I have done wrong in my life. (Take a few moments to ask God's forgiveness for anything particular that is on your conscience.)
Please forgive me. I now turn from everything I know is wrong.
I believe that Jesus Christ is the Son of God and that He died on the cross for me. I believe that on the third day He rose from the dead so that I could be forgiven and set free.
Today, I accept Jesus Christ as my Lord and Savior and

I choose to follow Him for the rest of my life.

Thank You for forgiving me, and I ask for You to come into my heart by Your Holy Spirit to be with me forever. I now receive that gift.

In Jesus' Name, Amen.

Congratulations!

You have now become a child of God!

At the back of this book, (Appendix I) you will find some helpful information on what to do next.

Again, congratulations as you start your new journey with God!

PART TWO:

Real Life Testimonies

Introduction

As I travel, I have found two types of people dissatisfied with Christianity.

The first group is non-Christians, especially those that are involved in some type of Eastern Mysticism, New Age or Wiccan type of practices. They have seen the supernatural power of the spirit world. When they compare it to their experience with the Church, Christians seem powerless! From their perspective, the Christian God appears to be weaker than the god they serve. Why would they change?

The second group is Christians and pastors. I have had numerous conversations about the lack of answers to prayer, especially for revival and healing.

If you consider both of these groups and their questions, you will note that the problems are the same!

The non-Christian sees no power in Christianity and the dissatisfied Christians experience no power or very little power in their Christian life.

I have no such questions. I have seen too much!

I have seen the Word of God and the power of God to set people free!

I have found that the Book of Acts is still happening today! God still saves today, He still heals today and He still baptizes believers with power. The Bible says it – I believe it and God does it!

In the Bible we find Jesus giving instructions to His disciples. He called his disciples and gave them authority and power over evil spirits and sickness and disease:

> And when He *(Jesus)* had called His twelve disciples to Him, **He gave them power over unclean spirits, to cast them out, and to heal all kinds of sickness and all kinds of disease.**
> - Matthew 10:1

After Jesus was crucified and was raised from the dead, He gave these instructions to His disciples in Matthew 28:19-20:

> **"Go therefore and make disciples of all the nations,** baptizing them in the name of the Father and of the Son and of the Holy Spirit, **teaching them to observe all things that I have commanded you;** and lo, I am with you always, even to the end of the age." Amen.

According to this scripture, we can see that Jesus was instructing His disciples to teach the same things to others that He had taught them. We can see they understood His instructions by looking at the Book of Acts. We see them doing exactly what Jesus told them to do. They went preaching, teaching and healing the sick!

We even see a deacon, whose name was Philip, also preaching and healing the sick in Acts chapter 8:

Then **Philip** went down to the city of Samaria and preached Christ to them. **And the multitudes with one accord heeded the things spoken by Philip, hearing and seeing the miracles which he did.**

For unclean spirits, crying with a loud voice, came out of many who were possessed; **and many who were paralyzed and lame were healed.**

- Acts 8:5-7

When we read these words from the Bible, we have been "educated" to believe that this happened over 2,000 years ago and this type of ministry doesn't happen anymore!

As a missionary who has traveled to many countries, I have experienced firsthand the healing and deliverance ministry of Jesus Christ.

One of the characteristics of revival or spiritual renewal has been the proclaiming and teaching of the Word of God, followed by God confirming His message with signs, wonders and miracles. The early Church understood this:

Acts 4:29-30
Now, Lord, look on their threats, and grant to Your servants that with all boldness they may speak Your word, **by stretching out Your hand to heal, and that signs and wonders may be done through the name of Your holy Servant Jesus."**

I am glad to be able to say that this same power of the Holy Spirit has been seen at Open Door. Here is a testimony we received at the church:

"I was born with deformities in my back. Scoliosis and a missing bone in my tail bone. For as long as I can remember, I have had back pain. The older I have gotten, the worse the pain has gotten.

I spent many years working long hours constantly on my feet. The pain got really bad. I would come home from work and would sit. It was excruciating to walk or do anything. Tears would well up in my eyes from the pain.

We have a two-story house and I would have to crawl upstairs to go to bed. But I still worked every day.

I went to many doctors (family doctor, pain clinic, neurosurgeon, physical therapy three different times). I have been on all kinds of medication. Muscle relaxers, narcotics, I've had injections in my spine to relieve pain. My neurosurgeon said that they could do surgery, but no guarantee of any pain relief. I thought, "Well that's silly to go through a surgery without any guarantee of improvement." So I said, "Give me a year and see what happens."

So all of this was going on and then the day before Thanksgiving 2009 at work, I had my first vertigo attack. It was like the worst dizziness you could imagine. I went to the ER and they sent me home with medicine for motion sickness.

Every few months during 2010, I would have this loud machine noise in my left ear and I would lose my hearing. I would go to see my family doctor and he would say I had an ear infection and prescribe antibiotics and send me home.

On Halloween of 2010, I got vertigo again. This time my husband went to the store and bought some motion sickness medicine, but my dizziness would not go away.

I went to my family doctor again and he sent me to an ENT. They did a lot of testing; hearing and balance testing. When I went back for my results, I finally thought we were going to get some answers. This was December 2010. The ENT told me that they would have to send me to an ear specialist in KC [Kansas City]. I started crying, saying, "There's nothing you can do for me in the meantime?" All they did was give me some nasal spray. It didn't help.

I was in a whirlwind. My life had changed so much. I go to the doctor for help and I'm not getting any.

I had an appointment in January 2011 with a doctor in KC. In the meantime, it seemed like I was dizzy all the time. By this time, I was only working two days a week and that was a struggle. I went to KC, the doctor ordered an MRI on my brain to rule out any major problems.

The MRI was negative, and based on that and my symptoms, I was diagnosed with Meniere's disease which is an inner ear disorder that affect balance and hearing. My balance nerve lost 40% of its ability. So I guess that's why I was dizzy a lot. There is no cure but it's not fatal. Surgery is an option but I would lose my hearing permanently. Right now, my hearing fluctuates so there are times when it is better.

My doctor prescribed a low-sodium diet and a migraine diet and sent me home to manage it.

I quit work in January 2011 and I really don't remember too much about that year. I was dizzy most of the time and slept a lot.

I would usually have a couple days a month when I felt

really good. My husband and I would try to do things that we liked to do and shove as much as we could in the good days. On the bad days, I could barely function. He would have to help me walk from room to room. I had a lot of dark days.

We met with Pastor David and Pamela in May 2012. It was a pretty good day for me. I wasn't dizzy but my hearing was pretty bad. I had pain in my back, but I always had pain so that was normal for me.

I remember them asking me what I knew about Jesus. It was so loud that I really couldn't hear and my back was really hurting.

After eating, we left and were in the parking lot. Pastor David and Pamela asked if they could pray with me. They said that Jesus loves me and we are not supposed to be sick.

We prayed and Pastor David asked me to walk around. My pain was a little better, but not much. We said our goodbyes and my husband said we would like to visit the church. June 3rd was our first time at Open Door. I was prayed for again. I remember being dizzy.

On June 17th, I was compelled to go to the front and ask Jesus into my heart. Since then, I think I have been prayed for over a dozen times and little by little I've been getting better.

Today as I stand here, my back pain is minimal. There are days when there is no pain. My hearing still comes and goes. I've had maybe three vertigo attacks in the last 9 months.

I know that I am healed through the Blood of Jesus. My heart knows it. It's my mind that is still struggling but the

Lord is working on that too.

My husband tells me all the time how much different I am today than before. I have so much joy it's always trying to burst out.

Jesus says that He does not change. He is the same yesterday, today and forever.

If He can do this for me, then He can change anyone's life."

And from Bolckow, the full Gospel of forgiveness and healing through Jesus Christ has also touched India and England! Here is a testimony from England that occurred during a mission trip in August 2017.

My name is Jenny and I live in Somerset, England.

Six and a half years ago I became ill with severe pain in my lower back. Up until now, I have received attempts to treat this with pain-killing drugs and injections. I have been admitted to hospital for doctors to try different ways to control the pain. The only diagnosis I was given was bursitis.

Two weeks ago, a consultant administered an injection in my back with the comment that it was probably the last hope of any relief for me.

A friend of mine (Janet) has told me on several occasions that her son David, who was a pastor in America, had told her about the amazing amount of healing that God was doing in his church.

When my friend told me that David was coming to

England for a short time and was planning to speak at Holy Trinity Church, I decided to accept their invitation.

While listening to his talk, although I was in agony sitting in a chair for a long time, I was determined to speak to David when he had finished speaking.

I told his mum and marched her down the aisle of the church to tell him about my pain and ask for help.

David talked to me about my Christian faith and my trust that Jesus died for me on the cross, which was not new to me and I was able to say that I believed this. He then talked about healing and did I realize that by Jesus' stripes I was healed, (two thousand-ish years ago), at the same time that I was saved. The answer was no, I did know the scripture but had not understood it.

We stood at the front of the church, and while David prayed with me my pain was gone. Hallelujah!

I went home saying thank you God over and over again. Praise God, it has never come back.

Thank you, Lord. Amen.

The following chapters are some of the testimonies that we have received over the last ten years, of the many miracles God has done through this small church in a small town called Bolckow.

We at Open Door, pray that you will find hope, help and healing as you read these true stories of real people that had encounters with the Living God.

We believe if God can touch them, He can touch you too.

We pray they will bless you and help build your faith in a God who still forgives and heals today.

Chapter 6

Invitation Leads to Healings

A Personal Testimony

Our journey with the Holy Spirit began many years ago when we attended a seminar on the Holy Spirit and were baptized in the Spirit followed by speaking in tongues. We attended a church in St. Joe but prayed earnestly for a Spirit-filled church in our area.

One day while Sharon was working at the Post Office, Pastor David came in to leave a poster telling about a movie the church was sponsoring.

We talked about Open Door Christian Center and he invited us to come see. It seemed very hard to make a move to another church, especially in Bolckow. Later, Pastor David came into the Post Office and invited us a second time. Being hard-headed and not knowing many people in that area, we took our time in deciding on a move.

Then in the summer of 2014 we were invited to church

by Pam and Lloyd S., but we had a wedding that weekend and could not go. After a second invitation from them, we finally made a decision and went to church in February of 2015. This was only about seven years after the first invitation from Pastor David.

WOW! Why didn't we make this move years ago. Who knows – maybe it was our stubbornness or maybe God's timing. What a blessing it has been!

The second week we attended (February 2015) Bob went forward for healing of his back. Within a month, his back was healed. Praise the Lord!

During the revival in September 2015, Pastor David was praying for healing for others. He stopped and said to the congregation that someone's hearing was being restored. Bob claimed that and took out his hearing aids. We didn't tell anyone for a few days. Bob has not worn his hearing aids since that day – September 23, 2015. Praise the Lord!

Sharon went forward for healing of high blood pressure on September 24, 2015 and now during this winter (February, 2016) has seen a drop in her blood pressure. Praise the Lord!

On September 26, 2015 Pastor David asked for anyone who wanted more of the Holy Spirit to come forward for prayer. Bob went forward and was refilled, plus received the gift of healing. Later that night, he prayed for Sharon to sleep soundly and God answered that prayer. Praise the Lord!

Bob has used the gift of healing on many occasions, including praying for our neighbor for healing of tongue cancer. On September 27, 2015 he prayed for our neighbor and the next day the doctor told him the cancer was smaller. Also, the neighbor noticed the lymph node in his neck was gone. Praise the Lord!

Sharon had been sick with the stomach flu on February 16, 2016 and was in so much pain we decided she should get to the ER. Before we left, Pastor David called to see how she was feeling since she had missed church on the previous Sunday.

He prayed with her and had Bob lay hands on her. Sharon said it felt like fire coming out of Bob's hand. The pain was gone momentarily but soon returned and she was stomach sick.

When Pastor David called he said she should just rest and he would check in about three hours. She went to sleep and slept very hard. At 5 pm she woke up and had no pain, not sick at all. Praise the Lord!

To be continued...

Bob and Sharon G.
Rosendale, Missouri

Chapter 7

Healed from the Effects of Chemo

A Personal Testimony

My husband and I were on a mission. After 21 years of living in Minnesota, away from our family, Gary retired and we came home to Missouri. We settled in the country and began attending a small church in a little town eleven miles from home.

The people loved God and loved each other and the pastor taught us in the Word of God and showed us Jesus by the life he led.

But now that we were getting older we were also wanting more – you see, we had read the book of Acts and we saw the early Church wasn't content with anything less than doing what Jesus did – healing the sick, delivering people from the grasp of the devil, even raising the dead.

This church had waited like Jesus instructed for the power that was poured out at Pentecost so they could do these things.

Rather than stay in the little church we loved, we decided if this church existed we were going to search until we found it.

After four years of visiting many churches, we were ready to give up.

One day, my husband Gary and his best friend and fishing buddy, were enjoying a day on the lake. As Gary was sharing his frustration over not finding the church where the Lord wanted us, his friend told him about this church in the town of Bolckow. This was 30 minutes from our house but we thought we'd check it out.

It was mid-December and I thought our first visit would surely be our last. Gary was looking forward to hearing this pastor preach, but when the service started we realized that morning was the children's Christmas play.

Well, you'd just have to know Gary to believe what came next! He says, "I'm leaving!" I said, "Well we can't just get up and walk out, that is rude!" As he got up and left, I followed as it was 30 miles home.

On the way home he says, "We'll go back in January and try again." I thought, "No way am I going back, it's just too embarrassing." But we did.

After that January service we have hardly missed a service. We loved the people. It was a small church and they made us feel so welcome. Pastor David Page took time to visit with us and share the mission of this small group of believers.

From the first time we heard him preach and experienced the service where the Holy Spirit's presence was so evident, we knew we'd found what we'd been looking for. It is truly a church living the book of Acts. Pastor David's messages teach, encourage and challenge us.

We had been attending for a few months when the invitation was given for those who needed healing to come forward.

I decided this would be my morning. After chemo treatments years before, my joints in my toes were so painful and I couldn't bend them. That morning I just knew I'd be healed. The pastor prayed then told me to do what I couldn't do before. I raised up and down on my toes and there was no pain. That was five years ago and I'm still pain-free.

In the spring of 2009, my dear daughter-in-law was diagnosed with cancer. The battle for a cure continued until August 2012. We encouraged them to come to church and be prayed for. By this time, at 43 years old, she was diagnosed as stage 4 cancer with not much hope.

Different chemo had been tried for years but the cancer kept spreading. After Pastor David prayed for her the following week, they decided to try one more different chemo treatment. In six weeks, she was pronounced cancer-free. It's been five years of being healed. The Lord uses prayer and doctors and we are so grateful.

We love our Pastor David and Pam, his dear wife. This small part of the body of Christ is growing spiritually and in greater numbers of people. Our eyes are on Jesus to see what He will do next – to bring many into a born-again relationship with Him – healing the sick, deliverance from the enemy.

Connie F.
Savannah, Missouri

Chapter 8

"God Knew I Loved Horror Movies"

A Personal Testimony

I've always believed in God. So many times through the years I have picked up a Bible and tried reading it.

I wanted to know what God had to say to us. But each time I laid it back down not understanding anything I read.... so I prayed...God, you know I want to know you but I don't understand what I'm reading...so please send someone to lead me to you... or let me bump into someone that directs me to the church you want me to go to.

So, through the years as people invited me to their church, I went because that could have been God answering my prayers.

It didn't matter what religion, I didn't think there was really any difference. Yes, each church did different things like stockpile food or tried to teach us women how to be better wives, but they ALL believed in God and we all know there is only one God. (And that teaching on being a better wife, well I couldn't get out of that one fast enough)!

Well in 2010, I was working at the Bolckow Post Office and a customer walks in and says he would like to purchase 200 stamps.

I smiled because I didn't think I had 200 stamps... I told him I didn't know if I had that many but would give him what I had. He said that would be fine.

He started putting the stamps on some kind of post card. I don't know if he was having trouble peeling the stamps off the paper or if he was just a slow worker. So I asked him could I help him, thinking I need to get him out of here so I could go back to reading my book. He was happy to let me help.

As we are putting the stamps on the post cards, he mentions that he is the pastor at Open Door Christian Center just down the road.

I said, "Oh really, I didn't even know there was a church down there".

He said it's the old high school. (So now I take a better look at him.)

He didn't look like any pastor I had ever seen before, messed hair, jean shorts and he talks funny.... He asked if I go to church.

I said, "I have visited a few but to be honest with you, I don't understand half of what the preacher is talking about and it's boring." I told him I believe in God and I have tried reading the Bible but I don't understand that either.

We started talking and I started to ask some questions and he demonstrated the message of the Gospel by using the door way in the post office. He said that I was on one side and all I had to do was walk through. (He made it look easy as he kept walking through the doorway back and forth.)

Well, I wasn't sure I wanted to walk through; yes, I wanted to know God and understand his word and the pastor made it look easy, but from what I knew of people that went to church you have to be soft-spoken and give up everything that is fun.

So I said, "Well to be honest with you Pastor, I know that gambling is a sin and I love bingo and that is gambling. And I am not ready to give that up." (Even though I hadn't been to bingo in many years.)

There were other things on my mind I didn't want to give up, but bingo was just entertainment, so [I thought] he would think, Well, she isn't that bad a sinner, she just likes to have fun.

He said, "That's okay Laurie, I like bingo too!" And I thought, if he plays bingo, it must be okay because pastors know the Bible.

As he began to leave, he said, "Well, if you want to stop by the church after work, I will get some materials together for you that may help." I said, Okay, I would stop by.

While I was there getting the materials, he asked if I would come and check out the church some Sunday. I told him I would, as long as he was prepared to hear my honest answer on how I liked it. (I was getting good at letting the churches I visited know just how boring it was, some even agreed.)

So, I came to church one Sunday and the first thing that got my attention was he remembered my name. Well, we started singing and singing and singing.... Don't get me wrong I like singing but I was here to hear about God, not sing.

So when we sat down and the pastor started talking he seemed happy enough, but would I understand what he had to say?

Well, the next thing I noticed was as he preached, it seemed like he truly cared if we understood. I thought he was just using simple words to help ME understand what he was talking about (since I told him most pastors don't make sense) but then he said "Let me give you an example" and he used a horror movie.

Well, now he has my full attention... I love horror movies.   He said, think of the worst horror movie you have ever seen. Now think of you in that horror movie for just 30 minutes, and then he said that is what hell is like, but you're there for eternity... Ouch!

Yep, God just used him to get to me! I knew right then God answered my prayers after all those years and this church was where I was to be, the pastor had no idea that I loved horror movies, but God did.

Like I said, I have always believed in God, but up to that point I thought I never heard from him and it was a one-sided conversation. But as I look at my past and the things I have gone through, He has always been there. And even though I wasn't willing to give up what I called fun sin, He was willing to answer my prayers even though I was only thinking of myself.

I was so excited I knew my life had just changed!

Well, I went out telling everyone God answered my prayers... God answered my prayers. I thought they would all come out running to find God.

I thought, the church isn't going to be big enough.

They looked at me like I had just fallen off the deep end. I thought, they know I love them and I wouldn't lie to them so why aren't they all excited about learning about God?

Well, after doing this for a while and no one listening, I got upset.

I came to church one day and told the pastor, People don't care! They deserve to go to the pit. You try telling them and they just don't care.

He told me, it's not the people we are up against, it's the devil.

I calmed down, but I was on a mission!

I needed to know everything about God and how I was to live. I mean, I've been praying for this for years and now it's here, I've got to get this down ASAP so I can help people ([even] people that don't want help), but I thought, Okay they won't listen, but if they can see God through me how could they not want Him? They would see how good He is!

So I started my adventure with Jesus to save the world.

How has this changed my life? I look at things differently as far as my life goes.

My husband and children were my world, and still are, just in a different order. But having Jesus in my life gives me a Joy that makes everyday a good day. There is nothing on this earth that can even come close to this kind of Joy.

The hardest thing for me is seeing people that I love being happy for me, but not wanting it for themselves.

Like I was, they are not wanting to give up things and yes I gave up some stuff (like my horror movies), but because I wanted to, not because I had to.

I have learned that it isn't my job to convince people, it's my job to spread the good news. I hope it touches their heart and they will seek Him for themselves, but I have done my part to the best of my ability.

I have learned that God doesn't send people to Hell; He simply honors the choice they made. You see, He still loves them to the very end!

And about all that singing I was against, I now understand why we do it and I love it!

Laurie R.
Barnard, Missouri

Chapter 9

A Miracle Child

This is the story of Nanette and Paul. Before the birth of their child, Nan came forward during a church service on October 23, 2016 and shared her story:

"Me and my husband Paul had been trying for about eight months...and, I knew going in that we would have trouble getting pregnant due to family history."

"We found this church and, one day Pastor said someone was suffering abdominal pain and, I had because I knew I had cysts in my ovaries and I knew that would cause trouble getting pregnant.

I came up here, he laid hands on me and the pain was gone instantly.

And then, the following week I came back up, prayed again, then I had an ultrasound and the cysts were virtually gone. Before that, I had about fifteen in each ovary and they were gone.

I think it was about a month later, went back to the doctor, found out I was pregnant."

At Open Door on April 30, 2017, we were privileged to dedicate their baby boy Beau, to the Lord.

Paul & Nanette P.
Maryville, Missouri

Chapter 10

"God Could Heal People in that Place"

A Personal Testimony

As I sit in my recliner beside my wonderful husband (while he watches his Dallas Cowboys) on this Thanksgiving evening [2016], I find myself pondering on all the blessings the good, good Father has bestowed on me.

Normally my thoughts go directly to my loving husband, beautiful kids and precious grandchildren... whom of course I am so thankful for, but this year is an extra special thankful time.

My thoughts tonight take me back to just a few weeks ago to a particular church in a small Missouri town, even smaller than the little Kansas town where I live. A church where I felt the peace of God even as we drove into the parking lot. A place where His love was felt by each smile that greeted us as we walked in. Words cannot express the Joy that overflowed as we entered into the beautiful worship and strength that rose up through the powerful teaching that the pastor gave.

What a glorious and refreshing Friday evening that was. It just doesn't get better than this..... or does it?

I must break in here to explain that a couple of years ago, I began to have abdominal problems. A constant ache was in my pelvic and stomach area. Then my stomach began to pooch. At first I just thought "Well, that's what happens when a girl turns 50."

However, it wasn't long before eating even a small amount became a chore as I became full after just a few bites. Having seen my mother suffer with ovarian cancer, it didn't take long to see that my experiences were very similar to hers. Also, knowing that symptoms of ovarian cancer are very similar to other non-threatening conditions and it usually isn't detected until the disease is advanced; it was difficult not to assume the worst.

After over a year of tests and seeing specialist after specialist, there was no sign of any disease... just a couple of bulging discs in my lower back, which wasn't giving me any trouble. So, not finding a disease you would think that would make a girl happy, not that I wanted a disease, but at least wanted an answer to what was happening inside me. I mean, if I'm going to have a distended stomach and it not be because of eating too much, there has to be something wrong.

I mean, I would have been ok with a pregnancy even though that would have been a miracle since a hysterectomy was done 20 years earlier.... since nothing was found, I changed my diet...... several times.... gluten-free, lactose-free and the hardest one was trying to eat five small meals a day.

Having to plan so many meals and prepare them consumed pretty much all my thoughts. This would have been fine, if I wouldn't have had to force down most of the food because of being full constantly.

So, here we are...... back to the wonderful Friday night service that couldn't get any better...... how wrong that thinking was. As we were driving back to the little Missouri town the next night to experience the anointing, I remember thinking, "God could heal people in that place."

Well, as expected, the same peace, love and joy greeted us as we arrived and entered into worshipping our God.

As worship was winding down, Pastor David said that he believed God was healing someone and for he or she to come forward.

In waiting he said that the Lord told that person He was going to heal him or her. I remembered my thought that 'God could heal people there', but hey, that was just me thinking, right?

Then the pastor said the unthinkable... "Someone who has stomach problems."

Immediately, I turned to look at my husband who was already looking at me with a big grin on his face, so up I went to receive what God had for me.

Pastor David and Pamela, both laid their hands on me and began praying. I literally felt a warmth flow through me beginning in my abdomen. God touched me!!

After the service, we received some pamphlets on healing and we purchased some additional books to help develop our understanding of faith and healing. The distention in my stomach didn't go down immediately. But, I know He touched me.

Knowing I have a tendency to get discouraged, I immediately dove into the pamphlets and books.

These confirmed that God literally touched me and released His healing power in me and that how important it is to take every thought captive. The battle is literally in our thoughts. So, when a stomach ache comes or the distention seems more, I go straight to the Word and make my mind think on His words and not my thoughts.

Healing is truly a finished work that Jesus accomplished on the cross, just like salvation. All we have to do is believe and receive it.

It has been a process. Being rather spoiled and wanting things right now, I am thankful that God is working in me. I'm thankful that He is teaching me about the healing process and how to keep my mind stayed on Him.

The 'bulge' is gradually dwindling, my clothes are beginning to fit looser and comfortably again. But the thing I am more thankful for is His Truth becoming more true, His power becoming more powerful, His peace literally passing all understanding and His joy actually is my strength.

Does it get any better? Fortunately... yes! In Him, it gets better and better!

Judy T.
Highland, Kansas

Chapter 11

A Spiritual Awakening

Note from David: *Rusty Chandelier is the name of an antiques store in St. Joseph. Not long after moving to Missouri, the Lord led us to rent a booth there to sell Christian materials. It operated for several months. It was in that store that I met Claudia and her husband, Rick.*

A Personal Testimony

I had never met an English pastor. I never met anybody like him. There was something different but it also was...I couldn't decide whether to avoid him or talk to him. But he'd always come around the corner when I was working. And I'd work and he'd keep talking. And all he'd ever talk about was God. And tent revivals! And all the things, you know, about the Lord.

And every time I'd go [to the store] it was like, *There he is again.* Then he'd call us and I'd think "What is this deal?"

But it was God working in our life. He had something we didn't have. He'd quiz me and interview me about my spiritual walk. And about my husband's spiritual walk, and about our kids. "Now tell me how you were saved? Tell me all about this."

And so, for one hour, he'd stand there and talk. Then somebody else would come in and he'd be off to witness to them! Then he'd come back, I was still working and he'd come back.

We've been around five or six pastors in our life, but we had never met a pastor who was so *passionate* about the Lord. I'd never seen a pastor witness, and I'd never seen a pastor pray in a public place for anyone. And I was uncomfortable because I had never seen that.

So to me it was unusual and new. And a little bit...do I want to say, threatening? Because I felt like I didn't know enough. I felt uncomfortable sometimes, because, you know, the pastor of our church had never talked to me about my spiritual walk. So, Pastor David was unusual.

And I guess another thing is that he wanted to meet my husband. He wanted me to meet his wife. As soon as Rick met David, we were *instant friends.* Rick went with him to the men's conference in Oklahoma and we weren't even members of the church.

David talked with a lot of people in the business building, that were there. He was always asking them questions and caring about them. And trying to find out if they were saved, that's basically what he was doing.

And so, to be honest, maybe for a year, it was like "I wonder if he's there? *I've gotta go work, I've gotta get my stuff done*, I wonder if he's there today?" And then, you know, he'd call...

He'd call Rick, he'd call me and he was so on fire about this *place*. This Bolckow. Who, I have lived here all my life...and never had heard of that town. I didn't even know how to spell it. And he was talking about church in a school and a tent revival and a wind blowing over a tent, and all this was the Holy Spirit and I didn't know who *that* was because no pastor had ever told me about that... And just on and on....

And then he'd call, and every time someone was healed, he'd call and tell us. And I'd say, "Rick, it's him again. It's him *again*."

And then I'm sitting at the bank in the drive-up window and I had [recently] fallen and hurt my leg. He knew about my knee, and he called to tell me somebody else had been healed.

So he said, "How's your knee?" He was on fire because someone had been healed, and he was excited. And I said, "Well it's still bothering me." So he said, "Well you just lay your hand on your knee and I'll pray for you." I thought, *I'm in my car, in the bank drive-up window. Oh my gosh. Really?!* So I put my hand on my knee, he prayed, and it felt better. Got home, felt better and it kept on feeling better. *It's never hurt again.* And it was seriously injured, to the point that I couldn't hardly walk.

That was the turning point for me. On the *validity* of the healing ministry. Because, you know, no matter how many stories he told me, it wasn't real until it happened to me.

So then my girlfriend's husband in Kansas City, [his] knee hurt. He had a bad knee. We were down there moving furniture and he couldn't move it. So I said, "OK Jack. Kristi, we're gonna put our hands on his knees and we're gonna pray." This was shortly after [my knee got healed]. And we prayed and by golly, his knee was healed! So that was the start of a spiritual awakening for my husband and I.

And *then*, we went through the Ambassador School of Ministry at the church. But I think that my biggest respect was that in eight years of friendship, he never asked us to come to the church.

So through prayer and learning about the Holy Spirit, we learned that we were to be [at church] in that town I'd never heard of, the place I did not want to go to church, in the building I did not like. To go up there was out of my comfort zone. And I thought, in the beginning, their story was just too...odd. Because why would those two, come here? To a town I'd never heard of.

The whole thing, for a long time, was just different and odd. From our perspective, it was like, this is a really odd relationship. But it must be a God-one. It's been uncomfortable, but yet it's been pleasant. It's been a BIG stretching, for people like us, who are settled in, in a big church, and we just didn't get it for a long time.

But we get it now!

Claudia & Rick G.
St Joseph, Missouri

Chapter 12

Restoration through the Holy Spirit

A Personal Testimony

Shirley and I had been seeking the Kingdom of God for over thirty years in pursuit of the church.

As we would read the Bible and compare it to the organized church, we became very disillusioned to the point of withdrawing from fellowship and attempting to stay connected through a ministry via the internet.

Though we continued daily in prayer and reading the Word for nearly two years, we came to understand the importance of consistent fellowship with other believers.

Little did we know that a visit from a longtime friend was to be a divine appointment.

Pam, and her daughter, Dyan, had an idea where we lived, but did not know our exact address.

They were looking for us to invite us to her son's

wedding. I had just washed the car and was outside in front of our apartment drying it off when they came by and saw me.

During our visit, the subject of church came up and Pam was telling us about how they had recently begun attending Open Door Christian Center, which was in their hometown of Bolckow, MO.

It caught my ear when Pam said that the Sunday services were different from what she was used to, and that Pastor David was focused on the believers and equipping them for the ministry. Then she invited Shirley and me to come and see.

On my first visit to Open Door, I was refreshed by the friendly atmosphere, the Holy Ghost worship, and the teaching on the Blood Covenant.

Shirley joined me in a couple of weeks which began an amazing journey of restoration. Under the leadership of Pastor David and Pamela, we have learned more about the ministry of the Holy Spirit than we had learned in all the years prior.

Their lives are a living example of what it is to walk in the Spirit. In a short three years, we have come from a point of being discouraged and disillusioned to realizing that we have an opportunity at Open Door to be the church of Acts.

Roger & Shirley F.
St Joseph, Missouri

Chapter 13

An Encounter with God

A Personal Testimony

We started going to Open Door in June of 2014. After two weeks, I remember being sat in my seat in the sanctuary. We were in prayer after singing songs and Pastor David was speaking. I just sat there and I remember thinking in my head, "This guy's talking about me, he's in my head, what is going on", 'cause it was new to me.

I wasn't used to anything like that, I had been to church, but you know, it happened here, so....

I sat there and then he'd actually said, "I know there's someone here to come down to the front", and my mind was just processing it, and I kept saying, "He's speaking to me, I know the Lord's speaking to him, *to me through him*," and He was, and it caught me off guard.

So as we were leaving that day, Pastor David spoke to me... I didn't even know him, I was two weeks coming here and, he didn't know *me*, he just... I was going out the door and he grabbed me by my shoulder and he asked me if I was alright.

And inside, no I wasn't! I'd just received some letters about some medical bill... just random stuff that had come the week before... and Dyan and I, it was on our mind. And I just remember looking at Pastor David and I told him I was alright, and in my head as I'm walking away, it was like... Pastor David was speaking to me *all day*.

And we went home and it wasn't a week later, I finally told my wife, Dyan. I said, "What is this about? What is going on? He was in my head, he was speaking to *me* and I *know* he was 'cause I felt it. It was like somebody <u>sat</u> on my shoulder saying, *Listen*, or *Do it*, and this and that", and Dyan laughed at me. She said, "It's the Holy Ghost, the Holy Ghost is speaking to you", and I said, "It's odd. Feels funny. It's *new*." I said [matter-of-factly], "It felt *good*...." But at the time I didn't know to open up and speak about it 'cause I didn't know what was going on.

We kept coming back here, and my life has just changed...drastically. From going out and drinking to DJ'ing in bars to just being around the wrong people doing the wrong things... you know, I was getting caught up in the world.

I thank the Lord for blessing me with Dyan... She has been very positive to me. I want to be a better individual and I don't want to be the person that I used to be, and sometimes it's hard. But you just live life day-by-day, and I look at life completely different than what I used to.

It's not the same, I could break down and cry right now, I mean it's just, it's amazing, the transformation that *I've* had, inside *and* out. I mean, I wouldn't even... I don't know where I'd be if the things that happened to me while coming here through God... I probably wouldn't be alive with the things I was doing previously, and that's just the reality of it.

I was so caught up in drugs and addiction and... following the wrong people, being with the wrong crowd. And now I stand out, and I'm myself and I've got my kids... I just want my kids to be godly, I just want them to grow up in the right environment... I've got to be that role model for them.

I mean, that's my story and it keeps changing and it's growing... and I love it! I truly love it.

I mean, we're getting a house, I mean *my gosh*, I never even thought about owning a house before, but those are things I didn't care about.

God has changed that. And I *truly* believe that, and I *love* coming here to Open Door... I would not be anywhere else. Not looking for anything else other than God. 'Cause of what He's done for me.

My dad was an alcoholic, and that's where I wanted to stay away from, but I found myself getting caught up in it, just... I can't blame the people I was around, I was making the choice. To do what I was doing. But I remember my dad coming to my ballgames drunk... yelling, belligerent, screaming... I *hated* playing ball and I was good at it, I was on traveling teams, I did a lot of things... but he made it miserable and I ended up quitting it because of the way he made me feel.

But then divorce came with my parents and... I didn't see my dad much. But he was hurt, he was drinking, trying to cover up the way he felt. Then he became blind and diabetic and had a stroke that [put him] in a wheelchair, and my younger brother and I decided to take care of him. We didn't want him going into a nursing home. *That's* the time that I got to see my dad for who he was. He wasn't mean... he loved... He wanted more than anything to see his grandkids, but at the same time he knew he was blind because of the choices that he made.

It was one of the classes we had here... I broke down here because I *didn't* forgive him for what he had done, I held that grudge, even though he'd passed on... but I [finally] let it go. We were kind of raised by my older brother, and I respect him for that, too. Because he did a lot.

If I didn't find God, I don't know where I'd be health-wise. Because I'd still be doing everything that I was doing in the world. And not living for God. And I am now. [I have] a new job, in the tire shop, more finances... Dyan and I, we sat down after some classes we've taken here and it's helped tremendously.

Financial-wise, I can't complain. He's blessed me with finances... I mean, it's not anything that *I've* done. And I just want to keep going, I tell Dyan all the time, I want more... I don't know, all's I do is pray and ask, you know...

My life is so much different than what it was. And I love every minute of it. And it's because of God.

Jeff A.
Bolckow, Missouri

78

Chapter 14

Out of the Mouth of Babes...
Micah and Amie's Story

Micah's Personal Testimony

I always grew up in kind of a Christian mindset of a home and everything with Biblical morals.

And as I got old enough to drive and stuff, I kind of got out of that... started doing some partying. I never got too crazy but there was always something inside of me... I didn't know it then, but I know it now, it was the Holy Spirit conviction inside of me, [telling me] that I was doing something wrong, that something wasn't right.

I didn't ever really drink that much, even at age 16, I think that whole summer I drank five or six times. So, the summer whenever I started into the partying and stuff, I had lost one of my best friends... We were out partying and drinking and he had fallen out of the back of a pickup truck and ended up in the hospital for about seven days or so, and then he ended up passing away.

After that, I just kind of... it was almost like I died inside. I changed after that and I just wasn't the same type of person anymore and I wasn't treating my girlfriend, who is my wife now, the way she needed to be treated, but things got better after high school and after we got engaged and married.

Then as soon as we had kids, things changed again... It was a month after we got married and she ended up getting pregnant, and as soon as we had the kid, it was good for the first couple months, and then I just felt like there was a burden on me, like I wasn't able to do what I wanted to do, I wasn't able to live... you know, the fun part of my life was cut short because of kids and stuff like that.

Then I got into my new job and you get around people and you want to impress the people you work with, going to things and maybe drinking a couple, then it turns into more.

I remember going golfing on Memorial Day in 2015 and I didn't drink that much, but the river was out so I had to drive around the long way. By the time I made it home I could hardly stand up and I was supposed to be home to watch the kids so Amie could cut [a client's] hair. I was so sick, I couldn't do anything, just lay in bed, so Amie had to take the kids to her mom's just so she could cut hair.

About two years before we started coming to church, our son had come up to Amie when he was about two years old, and told her that she didn't have to be sad anymore, that God told him that He was going to help make me nice. He said God told him in his room.

We tried to go to a few different churches and it never did work out, I still was out drinking and just doing stuff I shouldn't have been doing.

We got invited here to Open Door for a healing revival service and as soon as I walked in the door, there was something I felt that was completely different to anything I had felt before.

I didn't know what it was, but I knew it was something good. And I saw people get healed. I'd never seen anything like that before, and I never really even knew anything about it.

At that time, my son was always having just strange things happen. [He was] seeing a shadow of a man and he was just terrified and had nightmares and issues with stuff that he said would be moving in his room. He wasn't sleeping in his own bed or nothing.

So, a couple we knew that had been to Open Door got a hold of Pastor David and Pamela and had them come over... They shared with us about a lot of stuff that could be causing the issues. We had dreamcatcher type of stuff and Indian spiritual stuff, certain movies, all that stuff they shared with us about.... (My mom and dad had always told us that certain movies could bring spirits into your house.)

So we started getting rid of all that stuff, and just started praying with the kids every night after that. It wasn't long after that my son was doing better and we haven't had any real serious issues since then. After about six months or so I think it all kind of cleared up.

It was probably a couple weeks after that, we decided to start coming here to church and ever since then, things started getting better, between our marriage and the way I treated our kids and stuff. I wasn't a very good dad, I wasn't a good husband and you know, it's really changed my life, not just the church, but I believe that God's put this church here for a reason, and put all these people here for a reason.

Something that happened to me last year [2017] since I've been learning more about healing.... me and my wife went to get material from a guy in Rockport. As we were loading it up he told us he was sorry he couldn't help because he had hurt his back a couple days prior, and it came to me that I needed to pray for him. I asked him if he wanted me to pray for him and he said yes and that he was an ordained minister and would take prayer any time.

He had problems with swollen discs and a couple vertebrae. So when we got done loading up all the material, I prayed for him, and the Lord took the pain from his back. [He said] it was still tight, so I prayed for the tightness to leave and the Lord took the tightness from his back. He bent over further than he had for the last few days. He was so happy and excited that he could go back to work.

I'm doing things I wouldn't even dream of doing, like going to India. I've always wanted to go on a missions trip but I always wanted to go for the wrong reason, like a getaway almost.

It was about six or eight weeks before the trip occurred that I'd figured out I was going, and I still had passports to get and everything and I was like, there's no way. But I'd talked to Pastor David after service and I figured out that everything I was feeling as he was telling me, the persecution that happens and stuff, I had no uneasy feelings, so I knew it was from God and it was right.

I was wanting to go for the right reason, to see how God works through Pastor David's life but also through my own. And just the power of Jesus and all the miracles that Pastor David talked about, I was like "I've gotta see that happen".

And I just think that's a lot of the reason I went, was to kind of help me in my walk of faith.

I couldn't tell you the last time I've been drunk, maybe that Memorial Day. I've still had struggles back and forth, but I just wouldn't be able to do it without God, Jesus, and I give Him all the praise and glory.

Amie's Personal Testimony

"And be ye kind to one another, tenderhearted, forgiving one another, even as God for Christ's sake hath forgiven you." Ephesians 4:32

This verse has changed my life. If God can forgive me for all my sins, why can I not forgive everyone who has hurt me? Life is very fragile, and it can end in the blink of an eye. For many years I lived with so much hate and anger towards the ones who had done me wrong. I was always unhappy inside, along with dealing with depression. Never did I think that forgiveness would save my life.

When I was around five years old, I remember hiding under our kitchen table with my big sister, from the flying dishes, and holding onto my ears to block out the screaming. My dad had just gotten home from "work" completely wasted again. When he was drunk or high he was always mean and would take out his anger on my mom or us girls. He would constantly scream, slam doors, and throw things. He broke so many things that meant so much to my mom. *I could never understand why he was so mad at me.* Once I started kindergarten, my mom finally filed for a divorce and we moved in with my grandma and papa, but like every child in that situation, I began to question if the divorce was my fault.

After years of spending every other weekend with him and watching him drink even more, my sister refused to continue going. This was when he became very depressed which meant more alcohol. I got to spend my thirteenth birthday being adopted by my stepdad, because my real dad terminated his rights to my sister and me. This was when I started to feel the horrible feelings of unforgiveness. I did continue to go see him occasionally, but it always felt awkward, especially when he spent the entire visit crying, or complaining about my mom. Through the years we lost contact, except for maybe two phone calls a year.

Years went on and I grew up. I got married to my high school sweetheart and had two awesome kids! However, our marriage was not the easiest for the first five years. We were twenty years old when we got married and I was pregnant within the first couple of months. Being young and a married parent is not easy. I was one hundred percent committed to being a mother and wife. I took my son everywhere with me, he was my world.

My husband on the other hand, was a typical twenty-year-old guy who was not ready to give up his fun lifestyle and be home with a wife and kid. We did not know how to communicate well, which resulted in a lot of unnecessary arguments.

After a few years of his verbal abuse and absentness, I finally gave him an ultimatum – either change his ways or leave. This was the hardest thing I had ever done because he was my best friend. He decided he wanted to stay home, and I knew that meant I'd have to forgive him, but I felt like I couldn't. How do you forgive someone who had been so mean to you and your child?

I felt hopeless after trying to work on our marriage for a few months. I was about to call it quits when we got invited to come to this new church. Something about this one was different. My husband was anxious to go, but I felt like I was just being supportive by going.

After the first week, I could see such a change in my husband, and with every week after it only got better. I knew that this was the change we needed. God was really changing him, and for the first time in a long time I felt like I could trust him again. I forgave him for all of the past things, and we have never been more happily married.

On one particular Sunday, the pastor mentioned he felt that God was showing him someone in the crowd that was dealing with unforgiveness towards a father. I instantly started to cry because I knew that it was me. I had been struggling with this for ten years and did not know how to fix it. We prayed, and I knew I had to be the one to reach out to my dad and fix it.

After that Sunday, my dad and I grew closer. We would visit a couple times a month, and text often. He even met my children and fell in love with them. About a year into our new relationship, my dad was diagnosed with cancer. It grew rapidly, but he lived for eleven months after the diagnosis. I thank God all the time for helping me forgive him. Not only did it help me, but I believe he got to pass on knowing that I still loved him and had forgiven him.

After everything that I had been through with my dad and my husband, forgiveness was what kept me strong, and it let me be the bigger person. Yes, it was very hard to forgive them, but a scripture in the Bible says we will not be forgiven unless we can forgive others, and that is very important to me. No matter the situation, forgiveness will always be the correct way to handle it.

Micah and Amie B.
Rosendale, Missouri

Chapter 15

"My Left Arm was Instantly Healed"

A Personal Testimony

The exact date is hard to remember, but I believe it was two weeks before Easter 2012.

On Friday of that week, I was at work using a 10 lb. sledgehammer under a bridge. I was putting silt fence on the bottom of a slope to keep dirt from filling the ditch next to the railroad tracks.

The bridge was on 69 Highway, about a mile northeast of I-35. It was very hot that day, the exact temperature I cannot remember. This bridge was located over the railroad, between two curves, and the tracks were lined with trees on both sides.

This acted to effectively block any wind that may have tried to pass under the bridge. While sweating profusely and hammering 2x2" stakes into the ground, my right hand became fatigued and I was forced to switch to the left.

I am thoroughly right-handed and my aim is apparently not very good with my left. After the third or fourth blow with my left hand, I missed the stake completely, causing my hand to rotate farther than I believe it should. By the time I was able to stop the momentum, I heard a loud popping sound.

I have been injured at work before, which I believe would make me a marked man if I were to be injured again. In fear I was about to lose my job, I prayed as soon as it happened.

After a short break, I came back to the top of the bridge for lunch. After lunch, I mentioned the injury to my foreman, but played it down to not seem as bad as it was. His job position requires him to log any and all injuries, no matter how small; therefore, after talking him out of reporting it, I had placed his job on the line along with mine.

This meant I could not report it at a later date without both of us losing our employment. This only added to the desperation growing inside. I never sought medical attention; therefore, I didn't know the full extent of the injury. I have always been a fast healer and was optimistic I would feel better the following day.

After waking up early Saturday, I decided to go fishing in hopes of figuring out how to work through the pain. It turns out that it was a useless venture. I couldn't even hold the pole in my left hand to reel the line in with my right.

The only thought running through my mind was that I needed to get to church. I felt like I was in an absolutely desperate situation. I gave up on fishing after only the second or third try, but I was up early and had I gone home, I would have woke everyone else up at home. Therefore, I proceeded to read a book until around ten [o'clock], only to do virtually nothing the rest of the day.

When I awoke Sunday morning, it was obvious nothing had changed, [so] I was praying for a healing service at church.

Coincidentally, we did have a healing service and I could feel the Spirit moving from where I sat in the second or third row from the back. I was feeling slightly intimidated and didn't want to seem too eager or pushy to get prayer, so while others were being prayed over I simply stood in the middle of the aisle and waited.

At some point during the service, the pastor must have had a word I needed help, or could sense the strangeness of my standing in the middle of the aisle, because he proceeded to leave the others standing at the front to come pray for me. When he asked what was going on, I'm not sure he could hear any more than "arm", due to the emotions that I was spilling out all over the place. Once we began to pray, I could feel the Spirit all over me.

It is hard to convey the feeling to people who haven't felt it before, but here it goes. If you have ever been around plastic when it comes into contact with fire, you would have seen an intense and volatile reaction. The plastic doesn't actually burn at first; it simply shrivels up very quickly.

It felt like my skin was reacting in such a way and trying to get out of the way of the force that seemed to radiate from the inside out. It wasn't painful at all, but euphoric in ways that were otherwise unknown to me.

When we first began to pray, it was like the intensity of the plastic times maybe a thousand and it was nonstop, almost like my skin was constantly trying to get out of the way.

When the pastor grabbed my arm with his hand, the sensation grew locally by an unbelievable amount. It was unlike anything I have ever experienced before. My left arm was instantly healed and all I could do was praise God.

I was transferred to a job on a bridge in Leavenworth the following day. Had I not been healed, I would not have been able to perform the task of climbing over the side of the bridge to do any work at all.

Praise God for all of His miracles.

Luke M.
King City, Missouri

Chapter 16

Healing Revival Meetings

During the summer of 2015, the Lord began dealing with me about holding revival services. Since the last two revival meetings we have held have been in a tent on the ball field, I assumed that the Lord wanted the same type of service.

We went ahead with the planning and announced "Tent Revival Services!" to the congregation, to be held during that September. As time went on, I felt something was missing.

One day I said to my wife that I felt the September revival services would be focused on healing. She agreed and said that she thought they should be held in the main sanctuary instead of in a tent on the ball field. She had a picture in her mind of the website banner, so she proceeded to design it on the computer for me.

I saw it and my mind froze. "COMING SOON", it read in big bold letters across a blazing fire. "Healing Revival Meetings. September 22nd – 27th" "Are you sure?", I asked her.

Between that time and the time leading up to the meetings, there was such a battle against my mind. I knew it was the enemy at work, trying to convince me that God wouldn't show up and the meetings would fall completely flat.

I am excited to say that God showed up to renew, restore and heal people from various walks of life during those six services.

The following are just a few of the testimonies that took place during those services.

Neck and Back Pain Healed

My neck and back hurt real bad and God healed me I'm not in pain.

Mandy L.
St. Joseph, Missouri

Sharp Pains in Neck Healed

First time I have ever been to a healing praise gathering. With the encouragement of increasing my faith I prayed and Jesus healed the sharp pains in my neck I have. Praise Jesus my Healer!

Rhonda A.
(Town not given)

Back Pain Gone

Tuesday evening during worship the Spirit of the Lord came down and touched my back. No pain [on] Wednesday. Came back for Wednesday healing services and my husband wanted Pastor to pray for me. Really I was healed Tuesday. But praise God. Thank you.

Mrs. Eddy H.
St. Joseph, Missouri

12-year-old Senses God When Praying

When I was praying for someone I felt hot prickles in my hand.

Kylee M. *(age 12)*
St. Joseph, Missouri

Teenager Experiences God's Presence

I was sitting in the back thinking about Jesus when I broke down crying and shaking. I felt tingles in my hands and jaw. I became warm and just thought about me giving Jesus a hug.

When the tingling start going away I kept thinking about him more and more so it would come back. I had this experience one other time but this time it was more intense.

Alexandria B. *(age 14)*
Guilford, Missouri

"Jesus Healed Me, Body, Soul & Spirit"

My first visit to this church was 9/23/15 during the healing revival. I had just watched a sermon on TV by John Hagee that day and Pastor Hagee was preaching on the Door of Hope. He was saying that Jesus/God is the door and that all we needed to do was open the door of hope and walk thru to a new beginning, a fresh start, a separation from the past and give you overflowing hope and make a way of escape for you, plans for a prosperous future and answered prayers. So during his prayer call, I acted out like I opened the door of hope and stepped through it.

About two hours later, a friend texted me and invited me to a revival at the Open Door Christian Center. This is where I received healing for my body. On the second night, I had no intentions of going back up for the call of healing prayers because I had already had my healing and I was sticking to that. But Pastor Page said the Lord showed him someone in the congregation was dealing with shame and I immediately started to shake and almost hyperventilate.

So I thought to myself, "You were wrong, you are going up there again."

Now I know in His Word that it says Jesus forgives us no matter what the sin is. But the devil steps in and makes you think otherwise.

So Praise the Lord, Jesus healed me body, soul and spirit in just two days!

And back to opening the door and stepping through for answered prayers "of finding a good place to come worship and fellowship in truth."

I have been praying that prayer for 12 years. And also I hadn't heard of the name of this church before the 23rd, but the day after visiting Open Door I was looking through some notes I had written down about a week prior to coming here and at the top of the page of notes I had written for some reason the words "OPEN DOOR?"

I think the Lord was preparing me ahead of time that this church was going to be a good place to go.

Staci B.
Savannah, Missouri

Delivered from Voices

I got delivered of Native [Indian] voices and voices in my head set free.

Also I was refilled and re-fired with the Holy Spirit.

My left foot had a pain in it that hurt all the time now it is gone and I am the healed of the Lord.

Keith T.
Bolckow, Missouri

Deaf Ears are Opened

During the revival service Tuesday evening, Pastor David said he just had a word from God that ears were being opened. I believe God spoke to me to claim that word. I took out my hearing aids and I could hear perfectly. Haven't used the hearing aids since and have been hearing clearly.

Bob G.
Rosendale, Missouri

More Healings!

As we come towards the end of this book, there are still more people who have received the touch of God in this small rural town called Bolckow. Here are a few more testimonies of the amazing things that God has done in the everyday lives of people who are connected to the church.

Shoulder Injury Healed

I've had a bad shoulder for several years. It kept me from raising my arm above my head and kept me from doing many things. I was in pain most of the time and couldn't sleep on that side at all.

While attending a Holy Ghost service at our church, we were praying for healings. We were praying for others to receive their healing and I was stretching my arms towards the people we were praying for, I prayed "in the Name of Jesus, heal her body" several times.

I felt heat and heard a little snap in my shoulder, but didn't realize I was being healed, because I hadn't asked for healing for myself.

I suddenly realized I had my arm outstretched and that there was no pain. I could move it all around.

I never said anything because I couldn't believe I had really received my healing.

I had been healed and hadn't even asked for it. I think that was a grace healing, I had the faith that Jesus Christ could heal and He did. I'm 79 years old and feel like a new woman.

He is an awesome God.

Alvira G.
Savannah, Missouri

Bumps on the Elbow Disappear

Well, I had these bumps on my elbow and they hurt really bad. We went to the doctor and she said that they would go away in a couple months, but I had had them for four years and they hurt really bad.

So we went to the skin doctor and they took one of the bumps to see what it was.

So we left and I came to church on Sunday and got prayed for. I went back to get my stitches out and they said I had a disees [sic] and they gave it a long name and then she looked at it and almost all the bumps were gone.

Skye M. *(age 12)*
St. Joseph, Missouri

Blood Flow Blockage Disappears

Blood pressure was extremely high on top end and normal on bottom end. The doctor sent me for tests which showed I had a blockage of blood flow to a kidney. I was scheduled to see a kidney specialist.

I went forward for prayer on Friday night.

The specialist ordered a more detailed test before he would see me. Had on week after prayer. [Test was done the week after I was prayed for].

The tests showed no significant blockage and blood pressure has been fine also. The doctor cancelled my visit to the specialist.

Carlene N.
Maitland, Missouri

Doctor's Report:
Major Depressive Disorder in Full Remission

I have been waiting till the right time to share I have had a total change like the Bible says "I am a new creature in Christ" in only such a short time (3 years 2014-2017). Jesus has touched my mind, doctors could not make up their minds if it was bipolar or schizophrenia or what was wrong.

Well to make the short story one doctor almost killed me and one doctor "<u>Jesus</u>" saved me. He has done much, much more than that. And I am praising and thanking Him for much more.

PS – Thank You Jesus! I am who I am because of who You are! Amen!!!

Carolyn G.
Bolckow, Missouri

(**Note**: *Along with her testimony, Carolyn enclosed a copy of a doctor's report that revealed her new diagnosis - "Recurrent major depressive disorder, in full remission".)*

A Healing Touch

I was just waiting for him to ask for prayer . . . and he said that . . . If I'd had any hair, it'd been on fire. And I felt the healing touch. Praise God, hallelujah . . .

Roger L.
Fillmore, MO

No Blockages and No Stints

After experiencing chest pain, back and shoulder pain at work, my doctor ordered a stress test which would increase my heart rate with medication.

I became ill and experienced chest pain like never before. I was admitted into the hospital for a cath lab procedure.

I called Pastor David and he gladly came to visit and pray for me for no blockages and no stints.

As I entered the operating room I was asked what kind of music I would like. "Worship praise music", I said! I prayed and complete peace came over me.

A few more songs played and just as the doctor started telling me that he found no blockages, the song, "I'm Alive" played.

God is good, Amen! I thank Jesus that by His stripes, I am healed. I know that my Redeemer lives. Thank You, Father! Thank You, Jesus!

Judy W.
Guilford, Missouri

"I was able to walk without limping!"

My name is Michele and I am from Topeka, KS. My parents attend [Open Door Christian Center] and had shared the many miracles of healing that had occurred.

Over the years, I had prayed many times for my knee, to no avail. When I was 20, I had an ACL replacement in my right knee. In 2011, I walked across a smooth surface and my knee completely locked up and I fell. The orthopedic surgeon said it was the worst knee he had seen on anyone under 65. I could barely walk at age 47.

I came to the church knowing this was my last chance before knee surgery and a complete knee replacement. I went up front and when they began praying for me, my knees went numb and cold. Then I felt the bones begin to move! I could feel my kneecap come forward and up and the bones realign beneath.

Praise God! I was able to walk without limping . . . which was another miracle because there is no earthly cartilage in my knee.

Michele C.
Topeka, Kansas

PART THREE:

In Conclusion

Chapter 17

What God Has Done!

I hope you have enjoyed reading a true story of the miracles that have occurred in Bolckow, a small rural town with a population of 187.

One of our ministry friends who travels to other churches encourages pastors by sharing the "Bolckow" story.

We truly believe that what God has done in this church, in this small community, with a group of faithful, Spirit-filled Christians, can be done anywhere.

To summarize:

The church was born in 1993. In 2007, God began reviving His church, God's people at Open Door in Bolckow, northwest Missouri.

During this time God has revealed His faithfulness, His goodness, His presence, His provision and His healing touch in so many ways.

By the end of 2017, with God working through His people at Open Door with the preaching and teaching of the Word of God and God stretching forth His hand with signs, wonders and miracles through the Holy Spirit, we have experienced the following miraculous results in the last ten years:

UNITED STATES OF AMERICA

In Northwest Missouri:

- Church membership has grown from sixteen to 120 and growing.
- Over 300 people have accepted Jesus or rededicated their lives to Him.
- Over one hundred people have received healings.
- Over fifty people have been baptized in the Holy Spirit.
- Thirty-three people have graduated from the Ambassador School of Ministry.
- One member led to attend a Bible college.
- The property has been upgraded so that it is fully functional as a worship center.
- The church is completely debt-free.
- In 2017, over 500 people were served at our annual Shine 'n' Dine Fish Fry.

INTERNATIONAL

Current support for missions:

- Africa – A ministry training center is supported in Kenya.
- Brazil - Open Door Kidz support a young Brazilian boy.
- India - 14 orphans in a Christian home are supported monthly.
- Israel – Evangelism to Jews by Messianic Jews is supported by Open Door.

The results from church-assisted mission trips to India, England and Bulgaria in the last ten years:

- Five people accepted Christ
- 476 people baptized in the Holy Spirit
- 410 healings took place
- 120 leaders trained through a pastors' conference in India, sponsored by Open Door.

It has been an amazing journey so far, with more to come for this amazing group of people who worship at Open Door Christian Center.

As I was finishing this book, I was impacted by how little I realized to what extent God had moved supernaturally in our midst. Our lives move so fast, it is easy to forget the good things that God has done for us. God is awesome!

I would like to thank everyone who supplied their testimonies and stories over the years concerning the healings and miracles that they received through the ministry. We serve a wonderful God!

Finally, thank you, the reader, for taking the time to read this book. *We pray that it has inspired you to seek God more and encouraged you that God is still performing miracles today!*

APPENDICES

APPENDIX I

New Life in Christ!

Congratulations on your decision to call upon God to make Him Lord of your life! Here are some important steps for you to take, following your prayer.

The first step - Tell someone.

Find a Christian friend or a good friend and let them know that you have decided to follow Christ!

This is an important step in your faith journey. We would suggest that the first person you share this with is someone who loves and accepts you, and will encourage you in your choices.

The second step – Find a Bible.

To help you grow in your faith you will need a Bible. There are many translations available. Find one that you enjoy to read. Sometimes, it is better to start with an easier-to-understand version, until you grasp the deeper things mentioned in the Bible.

Translations that we recommend are:

- New King James Version (NKJV)

- New International Version (NIV)

- New Living Translation (NLT)

Another option is a study Bible. This type of Bible has

study notes in them and helps you with understanding the scriptures. My favorite study Bible is "The Spirit-Filled Bible" by Jack Hayford.

The third step - Find a good church.

As a new Christian it is important to find a good church. This should sound simple, but regretfully, it is not. The question is, how do you find a good church? What do you look for?

The first thing to realize is that there is no such thing as a perfect church. The church is a group of people coming together to worship God and learn about Him. We must remember that all people including ourselves have flaws!

The real question may be, "What does a *healthy* church look like?" Here are some things to look for in a healthy church:

1. It has a strong pastor who loves people.
2. It teaches the Bible and challenges you to grow spiritually.
3. It equips their members to serve and minister in the church.
4. It has a loving atmosphere.

The fourth step – Get water baptized.

In the Bible, Jesus gave the original leaders (called Apostles) the following instructions:

Go therefore and make disciples of all the nations, **baptizing them in the name of the Father and of the Son and of the Holy Spirit,** 20 teaching them to observe all things that I have commanded you; and lo, I am with you always, even to the end of the age." Amen.

- Matthew 28:19-20

Later, in the Book of Acts, we see these leaders baptizing new Christians in water:

Then Peter said to them, "Repent, and let **every one of you be baptized** in the name of Jesus Christ for the remission of sins; and you shall receive the gift of the Holy Spirit"...

...**Then those who gladly received his word were baptized**; and that day about three thousand souls were added to them.

- Acts 2:38, 41

We strongly recommend that you get baptized as soon as possible, to fulfill the commandment of Jesus. The church you decide to attend will help you and guide you in this special moment.

Once again, congratulations on your decision to become a Christian. Welcome to the Family of God!

For you are all sons *(and daughters)* of God through *(your)* faith in Christ Jesus.

- Galatians 3:26

APPENDIX II

Open Door Christian Center

Statement of Faith

1. SALVATION

The Fall of Man

We believe that Adam and Eve, the precursors of the entire human race, were created in the image of God; however, they disobeyed God and became sinners. Through Adam, all people inherited sin's nature and consequences, and all are in need of a Redeemer. (Genesis 1:27; Romans 5:12,19)

The Plan of Redemption

We believe that Christ died for all of us while we were still sinners; He took the punishment for our sin. With His own blood, He purchased salvation and redemption for all who believe in Him. (John 3:16; Isaiah 53:5; Titus 2:14)

Salvation through Grace

We believe that salvation is totally an act of God's grace that is accessed through faith in Jesus Christ. No person can be good enough to earn salvation, and "being good" does not contribute to receiving God's love and favor. (Ephesians 2:8,13)

Repentance and Acceptance

We believe that, when people repent for their sins and accept Christ, they are justified through Jesus' sacrificial death on the cross. To repent means to be sorry for sins, but it also means to turn away from a sinful lifestyle. Accepting Christ means believing in Him as the only Savior. To be justified means being declared "not guilty" in regard to sin. (Romans 10:9-10; 1 John 1:9)

The New Birth

We believe that the change that takes place in people when they are "born again" is very real. They receive righteousness through Jesus Christ, and they are empowered by the Holy Spirit; therefore, they should have new desires, interests and pursuits. (John 3:3; 2 Corinthians 5:17)

2. CHRISTIAN WALK

Daily Christian Life

We believe that people who have been born again grow in sanctification—which means that they separate themselves from the value system of the world and embrace and live according to the values of the kingdom that Jesus proclaimed. As they do so, they increase in holiness, faith, power, prayer, love and service (2 Corinthians 7:1).

Evangelism

We believe that evangelizing and making disciples is the primary "business" of the church; every hindrance to worldwide evangelism should be removed (James 5:20; Mark 16:15).

Tithing and Offerings

We believe that tithing (giving 10 percent of earnings) and offerings (amounts determined by the individuals) are God's instruments to carry on His ministry, spread the Gospel, and release personal blessing (Malachi 3:10; 1 Corinthians 16:1,2).

Moderation

We believe that Christians should avoid excess and that their moderation should be obvious to others. Their commitment to Christ should be deep and sincere, but they should not indulge in or lead other people into extremes of fanaticism. Christians should be well thought of, balanced, humble and self-sacrificing, reflecting Christ's grace and character in all areas of their lives (Colossians 3:12,13; Philippians 4:5).

Church Relationship

We believe that it is essential for all believers to join with and become part of a congregation of other believers. It is important to worship together, observe the ordinances of the church, encourage and support one another, and work together to advance the Lord's kingdom (Hebrews 10:24, 25).

Civil Government

We believe that civil government is established by divine appointment; civil laws should be upheld at all times except when they are in opposition to the Word of God (Romans 13:1-7).

3. THE SPIRIT-FILLED LIFE

The Holy Scriptures

We believe that the Bible is the inspired Word of God; it is absolutely true, enduring, and unchangeable (2 Timothy 3:16,17; Matthew 24:35).

The Eternal Godhead

We believe in the Trinity of God the Father, God the Son and God the Holy Spirit. The three parts of the Trinity are coexistent and coeternal, which means that they always have existed and always will exist together; they are coequal in divine perfection, which means that no person of the Trinity is more powerful or more perfect than any other person in the Trinity (1 John 5:7).

Water Baptism and the Lord's Supper

We believe that people who have been born again should be baptized in the name of the Father, Son and Holy Spirit. Jesus Himself was baptized and instructed His followers to be baptized. Baptism also confirms that Christ is the Lord and King in each believer's life (Romans 6:4).

We believe in observing the Lord's Supper, or communion, just as Jesus instructed. This means that born-again believers take the broken bread and the fruit of the vine as a remembrance and celebration of the new life that is theirs because of Jesus' death on the cross and His resurrection. It is also looking forward to His return as triumphant King (1 Corinthians 11:24-26).

Baptism with the Holy Spirit

We believe that the baptism with the Holy Spirit is an experience that follows salvation. All believers have a portion of God's Spirit within them. However, being "baptized" means that the Holy Spirit is present in a new dimension. Holy Spirit baptism empowers believers to exalt Jesus, to live lives of holiness, and to be witnesses of God's saving grace.

We believe that those who experience Holy Spirit baptism today will experience it in the same manner that believers experienced it in the early church; in other words, we believe that they will usually speak in tongues—languages that are not known to them (Acts 1:5,8 and 2:4).

Divine Healing

We believe that Jesus Christ heals people who are sick. God does not change; He is still willing and able to heal the body, as well as the soul and spirit, in response to faith (Mark 16:17,18; James 5:14-16).

The Spirit-Filled Life

We believe that born-again believers should be people who pray and who allow the Holy Spirit to shape their values and behaviors every day; their lives should exemplify love, honesty and sincerity (Ephesians 4:30-32).

The Gifts and Fruit of the Spirit

We believe that the Holy Spirit gives ministry gifts to believers; in other words, the Holy Spirit gives people special abilities for ministry. These gifts will build up groups of believers and help them mature in Christian faith

(1 Corinthians 12:1-11).

Further, Spirit-filled believers should show the spiritual "fruit" that has been given to them: love, joy, peace, patience, kindness, goodness, faith, gentleness, self-control (Romans 12:6-8; Galatians 5:22-25).

4. THE AFTERLIFE

The Second Coming of Christ

We believe that the second coming of Christ is personal and imminent; we are as certain that His second coming will occur as we are that His first coming is a historical fact. No one knows the exact time of His coming, but believers will continue to spread the Gospel around the world until He does come again. At that time the Lord Himself will descend from heaven, the dead Christians will be resurrected, and believers will be taken up to meet the Lord in the air (Matthew 24:36,42,44; 1 Thessalonians 4:16,17).

Judgment

We believe that everyone will stand before the judgment seat of Christ. Born-again believers will be sent to a place of everlasting life, and nonbelievers will be sent to a place of everlasting punishment (Revelation 20:11,12; 2 Corinthians 5:10).

Heaven

We believe that heaven is the habitation of the living God and the eternal home of born-again believers (John 14:2; Revelation 7:15-17).

Hell

We believe that hell is a place of darkness, deep sorrow and unquenchable fire, which was not prepared for man but for the devil and his angels; it will become the place of eternal separation from God for all who reject Christ as Savior (Matthew 13:41,42; Revelation 20:10,15).

ABOUT THE AUTHOR

David Page is a missionary pastor from the United Kingdom residing in the United States. In addition to pastoring, he also travels, teaching and preaching in churches, Bible schools, and conferences.

David grew up in a home that modeled Christian morals; however, by his teen years considered himself to be an atheist. At the age of 30, a friend invited him to the "Alpha Course" (an introduction to Christianity). David decided he would disprove the Christian faith once and for all. It was during this course that he discovered that the evidence for the truth of the Bible and the Christian faith was overwhelming, and he had a supernatural encounter with God which would forever change his life.

A few years later, the Lord led David to resign his position as a partner in a successful insurance firm. Following much prayer and wise counsel, he left everything to pursue God's plan for him, and headed to America with two suitcases that contained everything he owned.

The Lord led him to attend Rhema Bible Training Center in Broken Arrow, OK, and it was there that the truth of God's Word concerning the Holy Spirit, healing and revival began to develop deep on the inside of him.

Since then, the Lord has used David in many manifestations of healing and deliverance. He has learned and experienced things about the spirit realm that continues to help him today as he ministers to others with the Word of God and the Holy Spirit.

For more information, please visit www.healingrevival.org.

Made in the
USA
Columbia, SC